NATIONAL GEOGRAPHIC

Ladders

THE SAVAGE MOUNTAIN

A Mountain Called K2

by Judy Elgin Jensen

AD·VEN·TURE
a daring and difficult undertaking of uncertain outcome, usually exciting and somewhat dangerous.

MOUNT EVEREST
(mownt EV-uh-rest)
China-Nepal border
8,850 m (29,035 ft.)

K2
China-Pakistan border
8,611 m (28,251 ft.)

KANCHENJUNGA
(kuhn-chuhn-JUHN-guh)
India-Nepal border
8,586 m (28,169 ft.)

That's one way a dictionary defines *adventure*. How do you define it? What's an adventure to you? It might be a camping trip or a visit to a foreign city, yet what's daring for one person might be boring for another. But some activities are so incredible, so extreme, that they would satisfy anyone's hunger for adventure—a voyage to the bottom of the sea or a journey into space comes to mind. Or an expedition to the Himalaya, to climb one of the world's seven highest mountains?

Mountain climbing, or mountaineering, is full of adventure. Look at the definition again. Is mountaineering daring and difficult? You bet it is, even for the most experienced mountaineers, and no matter how certain the plans, the journey itself is always uncertain. Things happen—especially weather. A sudden snowstorm can stop an expedition in its tracks—or turn it deadly—but even in the best weather, mountaineering is risky. One wrong step can spell disaster, thin air at high altitudes makes breathing difficult, and frigid temperatures can cause frostbite in seconds. These are just a few of the dangers of mountaineering.

What, then, draws people to such an extreme adventure? Some mountaineers enjoy the challenge of pushing themselves physically and mentally, some climb for the excitement and thrill, and some enjoy risks. They all enjoy the thrilling views from the top.

Most experts agree that one peak stands above all others for the challenge and thrill of the climb even though it's not the highest mountain in the world. It's the second highest—and called K2.

LHOTSE
(LOTE-say)
China-Nepal border
8,516 m (27,939 ft.)

MAKALU 1
(muh-kuh-LOO wun)
China-Nepal border
8,485 m (27,837 ft.)

CHO OYU
(choh-oh-YOO)
China-Nepal border
8,201 m (26,906 ft.)

DHAULAGIRI 1
(DOW-luh-geer-ee wun)
Nepal
8,167 m (26,795 ft.)

The first thing that strikes you about K2 is its shape. The mountain rises sharply from the surrounding land, forming a steep triangle against the sky, and its towering summit appears unreachable, yet that is what makes it so tempting to climbers. K2 is the mountaineer's mountain. Though shorter than Mt. Everest, K2 is steeper and more challenging to climb.

K2. How did such a spectacular mountain get such a simple name? The *K* stands for the Karakoram Range, which is part of the lofty Himalaya in southern Asia. In 1856, a British surveyor explored the Karakoram and at one point, he noticed two tall peaks in the distance. He marked them in his notebook, from left to right, as K1 and K2.

K1 was known locally as Masherbrum, and that became its name, but the surveyor knew of no local name for the second peak, so K2 stuck. Since then, however, K2 has become known by another name—one that describes how brutal the mountain can be.

Mountaineers have nicknamed K2 the "Savage Mountain" because it is so difficult and dangerous to climb. With its steep slopes, frequent avalanches, and severe weather, it's no wonder that only about 300 people have ever made it to the summit. By comparison, more than ten times that many have summited Mount Everest.

The first thing that strikes you about K2 is **ITS SHAPE.**

K2 is the highest peak in the Karakoram Range. The peak straddles the border between China and Pakistan.

Challenges of K2

K2 is not to be climbed. That was the conclusion of an Italian climber who led an expedition to the mountain in 1909. The team made it to within a few hundred meters of the summit, but the weather blinded them and did not clear, so the climb had to be abandoned. It was only the second attempt to climb K2. The first was in 1902 when a team of six climbers spent 68 days on the mountain, which wasn't their plan, but stormy weather held them back. Later expeditions tried and failed as well. Finally, in 1954, another Italian team succeeded when they overcame the challenges that await anyone who dares to scale the Savage Mountain.

FORCE

With every step, climbers push and pull themselves up the mountain.

Pushes and pulls are **forces.** Climbers use force when they lift their feet, plant them, and then push off against the ground—step by step they move upward. On a steep slope, each step requires more force than on a shallow slope, so the steep slopes of K2 require a lot of force and are exhausting to climb.

GRAVITY

The force of gravity pulls everything on the mountain down, down, down.

Avalanche! The snow roars down the mountain. The force of **gravity** pulls the snow toward Earth's center. Avalanches can trap climbers. Climbers can face other dangers because of gravity. On K2, in 1953, six climbers were saved from gravity's pull and an American climber became famous for his deed. Five climbers roped together were lowering a sick teammate, who was also roped to them. One climber slipped, taking almost everyone else with him. Amazingly, another climber was able to hold tight to the ice axe he had jammed behind a boulder, stopping everyone's fall.

WEATHER

Camped just below 8,000 meters (26,247 feet), the climbers' plan was to go for the summit tomorrow—but this blizzard isn't stopping.

Climbers might wear shorts and T-shirts at the base of the mountain, but up here, the temperature is a bone chilling –30°C (–22°F), and the blustery winds make it feel even colder. Talk about extremes! Storm after storm can pin climbers down in one place for days or weeks, which puts a strain on their health and their supplies.

WATER

Even with all the snow around, climbers need water.

The air up here holds very little water vapor, so it's very dry. The dry air, combined with the rapid breathing climbers do, can make them severely dehydrated and they could become unconscious. So how do climbers get liquid water? Do they eat the snow? Not really—they can't melt enough snow in their mouths to get the water they need, so climbers carry portable stoves to melt snow for drinking. If the stoves get lost or broken, the expedition may have to pack up and head back down the mountain.

It took over 50 years from the first attempt to the first successful summiting of this savage peak. Then 23 more years would pass before a second team experienced the exhilarating view from the top.

A K2 climb unquestionably defines the word *adventure*.

OXYGEN

At this altitude, the oxygen and other gases in the atmosphere spread out more thinly than they do at sea level.

High in the mountains, climbers struggle to get enough **oxygen** because less oxygen enters the lungs with each breath than at lower altitudes. Less oxygen can cause climbers to develop altitude sickness. If so, they can get throbbing headaches and feel weak, dizzy, and confused. Therefore, most expeditions carry bottles of oxygen with masks, but if the oxygen runs out, and climbers' bodies aren't used to the lesser amount of oxygen in the air, all they can do is head down the mountain.

Check In   Why is K2 called the Savage Mountain?

K2 '78

by Jim Whittaker and Jim Wickwire
excerpted and adapted by Glen Phelan

PROLOGUE

BY THE LATE-1970S, K2 HAD BEEN SCALED ONLY TWICE. IN 1978, THE NATIONAL GEOGRAPHIC SOCIETY SPONSORED A U.S. EXPEDITION TO K2. WOULD IT SUCCEED WHERE FIVE PREVIOUS U.S. TEAMS HAD FAILED?

JIM WHITTAKER,

TEAM LEADER, DESCRIBES THE ADVENTURE FROM BASE CAMP TO THE FINAL PUSH FOR THE SUMMIT.

For years, I had longed to climb K2. I had already scaled Mount Everest, the world's highest mountain. K2 is shorter than Everest by the length of two and one-half football fields, but its slopes are steeper, its weather wilder, and its avalanches more common than on Everest. For me, K2 is the ultimate challenge.

I had tried to meet that challenge during an expedition in 1975. We were beaten back by stormy weather, and I saw firsthand why K2 is called the Savage Mountain. But I gained valuable experience, and in 1978, I was ready to try again. I gathered a team of 14 climbers, some of whom were on the 1975 expedition. We flew to Pakistan in mid-June and with the help of 350 local porters, we carried nine tons of equipment and supplies more than 160 kilometers (100 miles) to the base of K2. That three-week trek was just the beginning of our adventure.

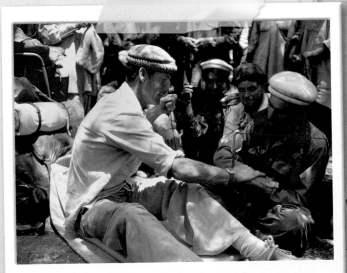

Jim Whittaker shows the head porter how to tie ropes. They will use the ropes to cross a swollen river between them and the mountain.

Porters trudge toward Base Camp at 4962 meters (16,300 feet).

The porters carry 25-kilogram (55-pound) boxes of supplies.

We established Base Camp on the Godwin-Austen Glacier at the foot of the mountain. It was July 5, the middle of the summer climbing season when K2's weather is the least dangerous, but summer weather still can be wild on K2. We even had snowstorms at Base Camp— a sign of things to come higher up.

I planned a route up the Pakistani side of the mountain, marking where we would establish camps and store supplies at different elevations. From Base Camp we hiked up the glacier to the foot of K2's Northeast Ridge where we set up Camp 1 at 5,640 meters (18,500 feet).

The Northeast Ridge presented the Savage Mountain's first great challenge—slopes as steep as 65 degrees. That seems almost straight up and down and one misstep could mean a fatal fall. Such are the dangers from **gravity**—the **force** that pulls everything toward the center of Earth. Some slopes were glazed with solid ice while others were blanketed in waist-high snow. We trudged carefully through the snow to avoid setting off an avalanche.

Camp 1
5,640m (18,500 ft.)

At such a steep angle, the **energy** of a barreling mass of snow and ice could wipe out all of us.

We made it up the ridge safely and on July 13 established Camp 2. Some team members went ahead to clear a trail through the snow toward the next camp. That made it easier to carry our supplies to Camp 3, which we set up on July 18 at 6,800 meters (22,300 feet).

Powerful blizzards kept us at Camp 3 for eight days. During breaks in the storms, I sent teams down to lower camps to haul up more supplies. That mostly meant boxes of freeze-dried meat, beans, vegetables, and fruit. It all tasted awful, but it gave us the energy we needed. Other supplies included **oxygen** tanks, which would come in handy as the air became too thin to breathe easily.

The weather finally cleared and we advanced. The route now was along a sharp narrow ridge with a sheer drop on either side. One wrong step would mean certain death, so we secured fixed ropes, like flexible handrails, along the ridge. Beyond the ridge, we set up Camp 4 just before another snowstorm hit. Hurricane-force winds lashed the mountain and we had to retreat all the way back down to Base Camp. Our spirits fell. Would the Savage Mountain ever give us a break?

Rick and John set up a tent that had blown down in a storm at Camp 3.

Climbers carry supplies between Camps 2 and 3.

Following behind one another in the cleared path conserves energy.

After the weather cleared, we struggled back up the mountain and set up Camp 5 at 7,680 meters (25,200 feet). From there I mapped out two routes to the summit. I had already chosen the four climbers who had the best skills and endurance needed to reach the top—John Roskelley, Rick Ridgeway, Jim Wickwire, and Lou Reichardt. This was our assault team. My wife Dianne and I would stay at Camp 3 and observe the climbers through the powerful telephoto lens of Dianne's camera.

Up at Camp 5, the four climbers decided to break into two teams and try both routes. It was September 2 and time was running out. Supplies were low. Everyone was exhausted. And we had to meet the porters at Base Camp by September 10. "It's now or never," I said.

After yet another storm, Jim and Lou followed their route and pitched camp 747 meters (2,450 feet) below the summit. The next morning, Dianne spotted two tiny figures advancing toward the summit through her telephoto lens. All day long, we tracked their progress and then, at 5:20 p.m., we spotted a flash of red at the summit—Lou's parka! They made it! Jim and Lou stood against a brilliant blue sky with all of K2 beneath them. For the first time, Americans stood atop the Savage Mountain.

Lou stayed only a minute or two before heading down and we waited for Jim to follow. Finally at sunset, we saw him start down. But we feared that he would never make it back to camp before dark. It was too dangerous to travel at night.

John and Rick had abandoned their own route and made it to Jim and Lou's camp, where they planned to start to climb to the summit the next morning. John radioed, "Lou's back, but Jim's still up there." Our hearts sank. Would Jim survive the night?

Camp 5
7,680 m (25,200 ft.)

Camp 3

Camp 4

Camp 2

Camp 1

JIM WICKWIRE,
ONE OF THE CLIMBERS, DESCRIBES THE FINAL PUSH.

The weather finally cleared in the wee hours of September 6 and we decided to go for it. At dawn Lou Reichardt and I left our mini camp and headed for the K2 summit 750 meters (2,460 feet) above us.

Every climb has its share of mishaps and luck. This final push for the summit included a series of small mishaps. Sheer luck prevented them from becoming major disasters.

After struggling with my climbing, I decided to use oxygen. When I opened the valve, I discovered the tank was only half full. Someone had brought up a used tank—small mishap number one.

We continued up the slope roped together in the deep snow. The lead climber had to push away a foot or two of snow, then pull and drag his leg forward. Every step required all the force we could muster. During this part of the climb, Lou's oxygen system broke down and he decided to leave it—small mishap number two.

Camp 4 was battered by driving snow and winds as it sat atop this ridge.

The team had to retreat and wait.

Jim and another climber carry loads of supplies.

They climb the steep slope as they push closer to the summit of K2.

Summit
8,611m (28,251 ft.)
Camp 5
Camp 4
Camp 3
Camp 2
Camp 1

Hours passed. Finally, about 4:00 p.m., we saw the summit 152 meters (500 feet) above. Near the top I waited for Lou, who was tiring quickly without his bottle of oxygen. At 5:20 p.m., we set foot on the highest point together—Americans had finally reached the top of K2!

The view was unbelievable. The setting sun appeared balanced on the smaller peaks of the Karakoram Range. Lou didn't want to risk altitude sickness from too little oxygen, so he stayed only a couple of minutes and then headed back down to camp.

I stayed on the summit longer— too long. First I buried a microfilm list of 4,000 names of people who had supported our expedition as a special way to honor them. Then I took more pictures and tried to change the film in the camera. My bare fingers became numb in seconds, and I gave up. I started down, but it was too late. I knew I could never make it back to camp before dark, and I hadn't brought a flashlight—small mishap number three.

A few hundred feet below the summit, I scraped out a flat area to spend the night. I lit a small propane stove to keep warm, but the fuel quickly ran out. The extra fuel cartridge didn't fit because of a broken connector on the stove—small mishap number four.

The situation was grim. It was dark. My oxygen tank was empty. I had no working stove for warmth or to melt snow for drinking water. And the only protection against the bitter cold was a thin nylon sack. I wrapped it around me and kept moving my arms and legs to keep my blood flowing.

Huddled in the thin sack, I dozed off. Suddenly I had a strange sensation of motion. Was I dreaming? Only half awake, I realized that I was slowly slipping toward the edge of the mountain. I dug the heels of my boots into the crusty snow to stop my slide, which worked, but I couldn't fight the force of gravity in this position. I had to wake up. I had to wake up.

Suddenly I snapped awake when only a couple of car lengths from the edge. I pushed myself out of the sack and crawled upward. The wind was pushing against me, but I made it back to the flat area where I used my ice axe and ice hammer to pin the sack to the icy snow. Then I crawled back into the sack and waited for daylight.

When the sun rose, I slid out of the sack and got to my feet. I was unsteady and confused—the lack of water and reduced oxygen was taking its toll. I knew I had to put on my crampons, or metal spikes that attach to boots for climbing on ice, but I was unable to do it. Then I thought of my family, focused, and strapped on my crampons and headed toward camp.

I met Rick Ridgeway and John Roskelley on their way up. I assured them I was okay, and I continued on to camp as they went to the summit. Lou was relieved to see me and I was relieved to have my first taste of water in a day.

Our ordeal wasn't over. That night, after Rick and John returned from the summit, their stove blew up. Rick's sleeping bag caught fire, with him in it. He escaped unharmed, but the tent was ruined—small mishap number five. We all spent the night in the remaining two-person tent. Luckily we had good weather for our trek back down, and we all returned safely to Base Camp.

EPILOGUE

JIM WICKWIRE SUFFERED MORE THAN HE THOUGHT DURING HIS NIGHT ALONE ON THE MOUNTAIN. BACK IN CAMP 1, A DOCTOR TREATED HIM FOR BLOOD CLOTS, PNEUMONIA, FROSTBITE, AND OTHER AILMENTS. WITHOUT THIS TREATMENT, JIM WOULDN'T HAVE SURVIVED. THE FACT THAT ALL EXPEDITION MEMBERS SURVIVED THE SAVAGE MOUNTAIN WAS A GREATER VICTORY THAN REACHING THE SUMMIT.

Finally . . . everyone was safe back at Camp 1.

Check In Which part of the 1978 K2 expedition do you think was most dangerous?

19

K2 2011

by Glen Phelan

Ralf and Gerlinde study the way
up to the next camp on K2.

An extremely dangerous climb makes a dream come true.

Gerlinde Kaltenbrunner had first seen K2 in 1994 from the side of a nearby mountain. She was fascinated by K2's shape—a triangle formed by steep slopes that merge at the summit 8,611 meters (28,251 feet) above sea level. In later years, Gerlinde would try to summit K2, and success came in the summer of 2011, when she and her husband Ralf Dujmovits led the International 2011 K2 North Pillar Expedition.

The expedition team consisted of six experienced climbers. Ralf, from Germany, had climbed all 14 peaks in the world that are higher than 8,000 meters (26,247 feet), including K2 from the Pakistani side. Maxut Shumayev and Vassiliy Pivtsov, from Kazakhstan, had each tried several times to scale K2. Darius Saluski, a Polish videographer, and Tommy Heinrich, a photographer from Argentina, had also tried and failed to reach K2's summit. Gerlinde, an Austrian, had summitted 13 of the 8,000-meter peaks, all without the help of bottled **oxygen.** The one peak remaining was K2.

The journey began in mid-June when the team left the city of Kashi, China, in four vehicles loaded with two tons of supplies—stove gas canisters, kitchen tents, tables, eggs, potatoes, climbing ropes, and more.

Why leave from China instead of Pakistan? This expedition would go up the treacherous and seldom-attempted north side of the Savage Mountain that straddles the border between China and Pakistan.

The team drove as far as the road would take them and then they switched the loads to a caravan of 40 camels and rode six donkeys. The caravan crossed rivers formed by waters of melting glaciers high up the valleys. The **force** of the fast-moving water could knock the donkeys off their feet, so the team crossed rivers atop the camels, who were amazingly sure-footed.

Five days into their trek, walking in temperatures around 40°C (100°F), they caught the first sight of K2's peak shimmering in the distance. Their goal was fast becoming a reality.

Days later, they reached the Chinese Base Camp at the edge of the K2 glacier. Another week of hauling supplies on foot brought them to Advanced Base Camp on the glacier with K2 looming ahead.

Seldom tried, the North Pillar route might be K2's most dangerous climb.

Gerlinde grew up skiing in the mountains of Austria. Her appetite for adventure led to a passion for climbing.

Gerlinde had summited 13 of the 8,000-meter peaks. She had one left—K2.

The expedition took the North Pillar route up K2. It follows a long ridge up the north side. The slopes are steeper on the Chinese side of K2 than on the Pakistani side. This route was very dangerous. It's no wonder so few had attempted it.

The approach to K2 from the north required three kinds of travel. The climbers rode in SUVs from Kashi to Ilik. They rode on donkeys and camels to Chinese Base Camp. Finally they walked on foot to Advanced Base Camp at the base of K2.

To Advanced Base Camp
Altitude 4,650 m

SUMMIT
8,611 meters (28,251 ft)
August 23, 2011

Japanese Couloir

△ Bivouac site
8,300 m
August 22
(Est. August 22)

CAMP IV
7,950 m
August 21
(Est. August 21)

△△ Tent site
7,900 m

CAMP III
7,250 m
August 20
(Est. July 22)

△ Tent site
7,300 m

PAKISTAN

CHINA

P II
) m
19
14)

△ Shoulder Depot Camp
6,250 m
August 18
(Est. July 7)

Middle Camp
5,950 m

Northwest Ridge

CAMP I
5,300 m
Summit push: August 16–17
(Established July 5)

The Climb

By the beginning of July, Gerlinde, Ralf, and their team were set up at Advanced Base Camp on the K2 Glacier. They spent July and half of August setting up several more camps connected by hundreds of meters of rope. The work wasn't easy. The route included vertical walls of rock and ice, and slopes were blanketed with chest-high snow. To make a trail, the climbers had to push aside a small wall of snow just so they could lift a leg to step forward. Avalanches often covered trails as **gravity** pulled snow and ice down the steep slopes. Then the climbers would have to clear the trails again.

After weeks of clearing trails, securing ropes, shoveling out campsites, and hauling supplies, the team was ready to go for the summit. The six climbers had become used to the lower levels of oxygen in the air. On August 16, they set out from Advanced Base Camp and reached Camp 1 at the foot of the North Pillar route. Heavy snow fell overnight so they waited a day to see if the snow would avalanche before they moved on. It didn't, so on August 18, they pushed ahead to Camp 2.

Ralf was afraid he would never see Gerlinde again.

Ralf was deeply troubled by the dangers of avalanches and he said, "Gerlinde, I am going back." He tried to persuade Gerlinde to go with him but she refused. She knew the route was risky but later said, "My gut feeling was good." Ralf was afraid he would never see her again. Soon afterward, snow ripped loose from the slope in an avalanche caused by the force of the climbers' steps.

The avalanche knocked Tommy upside down in the snow. Only his rope saved him from being swept off the mountain. He dug himself out, but the avalanche had filled in the trail between him and the other climbers higher up, so he, too, turned back.

Gerlinde, Dariusz, Maxut, and Vassily reached Camp 2 on August 19 and Camp 3 the following day. That night, like many nights, the frosted tent walls shook and snapped in the wind. The next day the team reached Camp 4 at nearly 8,000 meters (26,247 feet). At that altitude, the body can no longer adjust to the low levels of oxygen. Thinking becomes difficult and confused, and simple tasks take longer.

The climbers spent the afternoon melting snow for drinking water and sharpening their crampons to better grip the icy slopes. In the evening, they looked up at the summit above them. They looked each other in the eyes and said, "OK, tomorrow is our day."

The morning was clear, but the deep snow, stinging winds, and shortage of oxygen made progress slow. One of the biggest obstacles was a steep chute of ice. Far below at Advanced Base Camp, Ralf used a telescope and radio to guide the climbers up the chute to avoid deep snow and avalanches. After climbing for 12 hours, they were only 300 meters (980 feet) below the summit. They were exhausted. They set up a small tent and rested until morning.

The team looked at each other and said, "Tomorrow is our day."

Early on August 23, the four climbers set out for the summit. The snow was chest deep, so they searched for an easier route, which they found over some steep rocks. It took less force to climb at a steeper angle than to push through the snow. Soon they were on the small ridge that led to the summit. Dehydrated, Gerlinde took a sip from a bottle that she stored inside her suit to keep the water liquid.

Near the summit, Vassily said that he wanted to wait for his friend Maxut, who was a few minutes behind, and Dariusz was even farther back. They would all join her later. So Gerlinde walked the final steps alone. At 6:18 p.m., all of K2 was beneath her. She became the first woman to summit all 8,000-meter peaks without bottled oxygen.

Once on the summit, Gerlinde wanted to hug the whole world.

The tiny point of light below the top of K2 was a sign. It showed that the climbers had returned from the summit to the tent they set up the night before. Tommy took this photo from Advanced Base Camp.

It took two days for the climbers to get back to Advanced Base Camp, but they all made it down safely. They were hailed as heroes in their home countries although most don't climb for the glory. They climb to achieve a goal, to challenge themselves, or to inspire others. For Gerlinde, reaching the top of K2 was a life's dream come true. One of the pictures of her on the summit shows her arms raised over her head. "It's not that I felt like a queen," she said, "but that I wanted to hug the whole world."

Gerlinde was described as being "over the moon" with delight as she stood on top of K2.

Check In Why was Gerlinde's climb to the summit of K2 so remarkable?

GEARED UP!

by Lara Winegar

When Gerlinde Kaltenbrunner left Camp 1 at the foot of the North Pillar, she left her journal behind. She didn't forget it, or even drop it; she just didn't want to carry the weight of it. She knew that every gram counts when you're trudging through deep snow up treacherous, steep slopes. The more weight you carry, the more **force** you need to move it, so your equipment has to be as lightweight as possible. It also has to be durable—strong and long-lasting enough to hold up throughout the entire expedition. No stores or repair shops "just around the corner" on the mountain!

So, what does a well-equipped climber need to pack in order to tackle the tall peaks? Here is a small sampling of gear that experienced climbers wouldn't be without.

COMPASS tells in what direction north is and is important if the GPS fails.

GLOBAL POSITIONING SYSTEM (GPS) tells a climber's exact location.

GOGGLES protect against strong sunlight that reflects off the snow.

ROPES support the weight of climbers as they move up and down steep surfaces.

TENT AND SLEEPING BAG keep a climber warm by blocking wind and holding in body heat.

BOOTS protect and keep feet warm. They have an inner boot of foam, an outer boot of plastic or leather, and an insulated outer layer of waterproof fabric.

ICE AXE wedges into the ice so a climber can pull on it or pin down objects such as sleeping bags.

CRAMPONS claw into ice. These metal spikes attach to the bottom of the boots.

Check In Which one of these items would you most not want to lose? Tell why.

Discuss

1. How did the information in "A Mountain Called K2" help you understand the other three pieces in the book?

2. Compare and contrast the expeditions described in "K2 1978" and "K2 2011"?

3. Cite examples of the effects of forces such as gravity on climbers from "A Mountain Called K2," "K2 1978," and "K2 2011."

4. Explain how gear from "Geared Up" helps a climber handle mountain-climbing challenges such as blinding snow, gravity, and freezing temperatures.

5. What do you still wonder about mountain-climbing expeditions such as "K2 1978" and "K2 2011"? What would be some good ways to find more information?